First Facts®

MILITARY MACHINES ON DUTY

MIGHTY MILITARY ROBOTS

by WILLIAM N. STARK Consultant: Dennis P. Mroczkowski, Colonel, US Marine Corps (Ret.)

CAPSTONE PRESS
a capstone imprint

First Facts are published by Capstone Press,
1710 Roe Crest Drive, North Mankato, Minnesota 56003
www.mycapstone.com

Library of Congress Cataloging-in-Publication Data
Stark, William N.
  Mighty military robots / by William N. Stark.
    pages cm. — (First facts. Military machines on duty)
  Includes bibliographical references and index.
  Summary: "Gives readers a quick look at modern military robots"— Provided
by publisher.
  Audience: Grades K-3.
  ISBN 978-1-4914-8847-8 (library binding)
  ISBN 978-1-4914-8851-5 (eBook PDF)
  1. Military robots—Juvenile literature. 2. Armed Forces—Robots—Juvenile literature.
I. Title.
  UG450.S83 2016
  623.7—dc23   2015029652

Editorial Credits: Mandy Robbins, editor; Kristi Carlson, designer;
Jo Miller, media researcher; Gene Bentdahl, production specialist

Photo Credits: Alamy: ZUMA Press/Tampa Bay Times/Edmund D. Fountain, 17;
Getty Images: Justin Sullivan, 5, Win McNamee, 13; Newscom: WENN Photos CB2/
ZOB, 11; U.S. Air Force photo by Airman 1st Class Eboni Reece, 9, Staff Sgt. James
L. Harper Jr., 15; U.S. Army photo by Capt. Allie Scott, 21, Sgt. Giancarlo Casem,
Cover (bottom), Spc. Giancarlo Casem, 19; U.S. Marine Corps photo by Cpl. Sean
Searfus, 7; U.S. Navy Photo by MC3 Edward Guttierrez, Cover (top)

Design Element: Shutterstock: Grebnev (metal texture background)

Printed in the United States of America in North Mankato, Minnesota.
092015   009221CGS16

TABLE OF CONTENTS

MACHINES OF THE FUTURE

Military robots have awesome abilities. They do jobs that humans and animals once did. Robots make many tasks safer. They do repairs, move supplies, gather information, and find bombs. Some robots roll around on the ground. Others fly through the air. Nothing stops these mighty machines!

iROBOT 510 PACKBOT

The iRobot 510 PackBot is a strong, lightweight robot. It disables roadside bombs. It also goes on secret spying missions. The user operates the robot from a safe distance with a remote control. This keeps the user from danger. The PackBot also has a camera. It lets the user see what the robot sees at all times.

FACT FILE

PackBots are about the size of a small suitcase. They weigh about 40 pounds (18 kilograms).

REMOTEC ANDROS F6A

The REMOTEC ANDROS F6A is a heavy-duty robot. It weighs 485 pounds (220 kg). This machine can switch from **tracks** to wheels. This feature lets it cross any **terrain**. The F6A is used for disabling bombs. Because it carries cameras, it can also collect audio and video information.

tracks—metal and rubber that stretch around a vehicle's wheels

terrain—the surface of the land

MULE

In the past horses, wagons, and mules carried military equipment. But soldiers carried their own gear. A soldier's supplies weigh about 75 pounds (34 kg). The MULE can help with that. It carries up to 1 ton (0.9 metric ton). The user moves the MULE with a remote control. Soldiers in Afghanistan have used the MULE.

SAMURAI FLYER

The Samurai Flyer fits in the palm of a hand. The Flyer can be launched from the ground. It can also be thrown like a boomerang. This flying robot can **hover** for 30 minutes. Tiny cameras let it gather **intelligence**. The seed from a maple tree inspired the design of the Samuri Flyer. Like a maple seed, the robot has only one **rotor**.

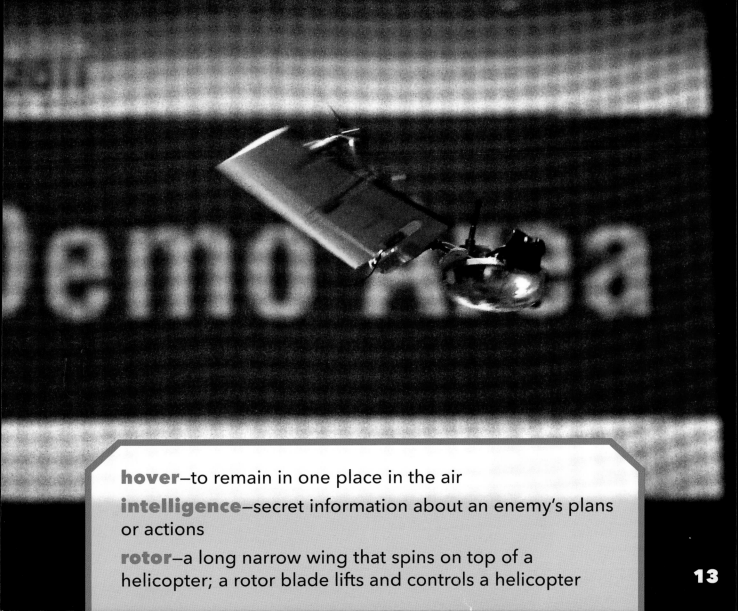

hover—to remain in one place in the air

intelligence—secret information about an enemy's plans or actions

rotor—a long narrow wing that spins on top of a helicopter; a rotor blade lifts and controls a helicopter

MQ-9 REAPER

The MQ-9 Reaper has shown value in both Iraq and Afghanistan. This **drone** gathers information to help plan military missions. It can also fire on enemies. The drone flies up to 230 miles (370 kilometers) per hour. Two people remotely operate the Reaper. The pilot steers. The other person reads and controls its **sensors**.

drone—an unmanned, remote-controlled aircraft or missile

sensor—an instrument that detects changes and sends information to a controlling device

15

DRAGON RUNNER 10

The Dragon Runner 10 (DR-10) is only 10 pounds (4.5 kg), but it has a big job. It can help a soldier safely check out a **suspicious** building. The operator uses a remote control to move the DR-10. This four-wheeled robot goes forward, backward, left, and right. Its cameras, microphones, and sensors send data back to the user.

suspicious—when something or someone appears distrustful

FOSTER-MILLER TALON

On September 11, 2001, terrorists attacked the World Trade Center in New York City. Rescuers used the Talon robot to search for survivors. They sent it through unstable **debris** to look for victims. A user operates the Talon from a computer. Its camera sees areas that would be unsafe for people to go. The Talon can also disable bombs.

debris—the scattered pieces of something that has been broken or destroyed

AMAZING BUT TRUE!

Military life is stressful. Soldiers depend on machines and weapons to help keep them safe. It's not surprising that many soldiers name their planes, ships, and guns. The same is true for robots. Soldiers in Afghanistan named a Talon robot *Danielle*. *Danielle*'s job was to search caves and canyons for bombs and enemies.

GLOSSARY

debris *(duh-BREE)*—the scattered pieces of something that has been broken or destroyed

drone *(DROHN)*—an unmanned, remote-controlled aircraft or missile

hover *(HUHV-ur)*—to remain in one place in the air

IED *(eye-ee-DEE)*—stands for improvised explosive device; a homemade bomb

intelligence *(in-TEL-uh-jenss)*—secret information about an enemy's plans or actions

rotor *(ROH-tur)*—a long narrow wing that spins on top of a helicopter; a rotor blade lifts and controls a helicopter

sensor *(SEN-sur)*—an instrument that detects changes and sends information to a controlling device

suspicious *(suh-SPISH-uhs)*—when something or someone appears distrustful

terrain *(tuh-RAYN)*—the surface of the land

tracks *(TRAKS)*—metal and rubber that stretch around a vehicle's wheels

READ MORE

Alpert, Barbara. *U.S. Military Robots*. U.S. Military Technology. North Mankato, Minn.: Capstone Press, 2013.

Clay, Kathryn. *Robots in Risky Jobs: On the Battlefield and Beyond*. The World of Robots. North Mankato, Minn.: Capstone Press, 2014.

Price, Sean Stewart. *Amazing Military Robots*. Robots. North Mankato, Minn.: Capstone Press, 2013.

INTERNET SITES

FactHound offers a safe, fun way to find Internet sites related to this book. All of the sites on FactHound have been researched by our staff.

Here's all you do:

Visit *www.facthound.com*

Type in this code: 9781491488478

Super-cool stuff! Check out projects, games and lots more at **www.capstonekids.com**

CRITICAL THINKING USING THE COMMON CORE

1. What types of missions would flying robots be better suited for compared to rolling robots? Why? (Key Ideas and Details)

2. What types of robots do you think the military should use in the future? What benefits would they offer? (Integration of Knowledge and Ideas)

INDEX